Elegy for a Butterfly

Images & Words
Neal Sehgal

ISBN-13: 978-0-578-41571-0
ISBN-10: 0-578-41571-2

For Her

on nights when love is pondered,
i spill ink across the palimpsest
and each time your name appears from the plash.

PROLOGUE

A LITTLE BOY FELL IN LOVE WITH A BUTTERFLY
WHOM HE HELD CLOSE IN THE CLASP OF HIS HANDS.
BUT MORE WITH EACH PASSING HOUR, SHE WOULD
APPLAUD HER LIMBS TO ENCOURAGE AN ESCAPE TO
BE FREE. WHILE THE BOY WAS INNOCENT, HE WAS
NOT UNSWISE FOR HE KNEW IT WAS A CRIME TO CAGE
THOSE WITH WINGS. SO, HE BOWED BEFORE THE
GREAT BLACK WILLOW, UNFOLDED HIS PRAYING
HANDS, AND WORSHIPPED UPON A WISH THAT SHE
WOULD BE SEDUCED TO STAY. BUT AS SHE ASCENDED
INTO AN ECHO OF HIS EYE, HE BREATHED HER A KISS
WITH A SIGH AND SAID, "ONE DAY, I WILL GROW TALL
UNTIL MY CHIN CAN TOUCH THE SKY AND MEET YOU
ON THE CLOUDS OF WHAT COULD HAVE BEEN."

the first time
i gazed into your eyes,
it was like staring at the sun.
now i know nothing else but you—
the last beautiful thing i will ever see—
blind to anyone else who could ever be.

she was sunkissed.
wanderlust for the hemispheres.
earthshine against her silhouette.
stardust in her naked gaze.

eclipsing all who came before.

beautiful for the moment she was here—
forever bittersweet in the ways i will remember.

i was born of the earth,
and she reigned the ether.
together as we fell in love,
rooted ourselves so deeply into the soil
that we bloomed far into the abyss of the sky.

holding her dear–
clasping her wings–
made me feel immune to gravity.
my feet touched the ground
but, my god, i was soaring.

i remember this one quiet summer night
when i laid awake as you slept beside me.

your skin was pearlescent
and your scent was sweet.

the flicker of your eyes was like
the waves of a flame in a fireplace.

the slow rise and fall of your breathing chest
was like an ocean wave beckoning me to dive in.

i wondered what you were dreaming of.
i wondered what story your heart was telling you.

i remember thinking that i wanted to be the hero in that tale
and that maybe, just maybe, you were thinking of me.

and maybe, just maybe, when the morning would come
that hero was someone i could be.

where did all those beginnings go? those frigid mornings of our bodies enlaced like two fleece blankets tossed about each other. those moon-soaked evenings of white sheets and red wine. of long hugs and locked eyes. of synchronized heartbeats and butterfly kisses. punch-drunk tongues and love-struck lips. yearning flesh caressed against curious fingertips. melting into me like warm chocolate as your back pressed against the frame of my bones. our anatomy in dalliance as i would gently trace a "u" with your hair and tuck the locks behind your ear, cupping the nape of your neck and leaning you forward into me as we came to breathe the same air. those moments. my love, where did those beginnings go?

i would try to catch your tears with my lips;
trip the trail they traveled down your cheeks with a kiss.

silence the quiver in your hands with the clasp of mine;
hold your sorrows sacredly in my palms
and pray them away to another day.

as you slept,
i would stand guard
at the altar of your tender feet
to protect your dreams
so that you were safe to explore them.

…i never knew what it was to love until i learned of you…

god made the air.
then he made lungs.
and at last,
just for me,
he made you
so i would know what it was to breathe.

it was as if each imperfection was a bijou hidden in the contours of you. asymmetrically perfect and uniquely your own. a vista of porcelain hills and valleys for me to explore – culling the parts of me you wish to give away. a supple garden of bliss to till and forehead kisses to plant upon your third eye as i dove deeper down into the depths of you. this terrain of your skin. i wanted to traverse it all and be lost there forever...

in all those thousands of silences,
did you feel my pulse through your fingertips?
because i felt yours beating through mine.
it was the rhythm of our souls making music,
and i could have sworn to the heavens
that it was the start of something beautiful.

everything about you was my scripture.
in you, i found the divine.

to me, you were a queen. elegant, graceful, strong. and i wanted nothing more than to be the one to whom you would turn to let your hair down. to be free of any expectations to be the kind of perfect that you were. i wanted for you to fall into my chest and let it all go. to be as unrestrained as you needed to be, so that you could arise the next day to present the world with your majesty. your magic. i knew you were too composed for your soul to breathe brightly. there was a tightening noose dimming its shine that i tried to cut loose with all the humor and wit god gave me. and so i would make jokes, tell silly stories, rewrite the drama of my days and turn them into punchlines. act a fool and play the jester. and with every atom within you dancing in my arms, you laughed. guttural and true. and when you would laugh, i would laugh because your joy was mine too. each chuckle, giggle, chortle, and guffaw weaved themselves into a soaring tapestry of sound. it was the song you sang that blanketed the night before it would awake anew. yes, my love, this is the music that still rings in my ears. the staccato in your voice and the reverberations in your cheeks as you so breathlessly tried to find your way back to speak. but i did not need you to because for you to lose yourself in me said more than words. oh, what a clown i made of myself in the hopes that one day you would crown me your king.

i never wanted to own you
and never did i feel you owed me.
i was just a humble servant to the fleeting time we had.
a master of nothing more than my own heart,
which always felt more whole
the more it gave to you.

swinging in circles,
it was a miracle
we ever came to dance at all.

orated in puzzles,
it was the oracle
who foretold our rise and fall.

hands held unified,
fused and forever mystified
by the bonds we forged.

but the waves came
to claim the wind
and drowned what once emerged.

the heart does not need the mind to understand itself.
in fact, the two rarely understand each other at all.

this dichotomy was what built us up to fall in love.
it was the very thing that tore us down to fall apart.

a brilliant confusion that, for the briefest of moments,
birthed all too much light into the chasms of our souls.

and then, it was a quiet death to a life we never lived—
forever nothing more than a dream in our waking sleep.

i poured myself into you,
and you drank me in.
fervid beyond civilized
in ways that broke

the familiar.

there i fell through,
paralyzed beyond repose
but descending all the same
in ways that obscured

the ascension.

i
tore down
my wall
to fall
in love
with you
and it was
the most
exhilarating
destructive
fortuitous
reckless
and
courageous
thing i ever did.
a thousand lives died
with my sights set on you.
it was worth every breath it took
and all the rubble of me that remains.

for the first time in my life,
i was not afraid to surrender
myself to the will of another.

i found freedom in holding her closer–
in the dissipating spaces of pitter patter
between our hearts beating as one.

i am an orchestra
of different strings.
limbs in legato.
torso in tenuto.
mind in marcato.
speech in staccato.
each playing its melody
in symphony to the same song
...
i wish you were here.

it was not a perfect picture of love i was after.
it was just you.
whether we came with a dented frame
or cracked glass
or torn corners
or sun-stained film,
all i ever wanted was you.
indeed,
we were flawed
but we did so beautifully fit in each other's arms.

i do not know
what scares me more:
that i will never forget you
or that i will.
this wheel of love
that i spin safe for you
is swarming with sharp edges
that is sure to bleed me dry
no matter
which way it turns.

in the clatter of a hundred talking,
i can hear your voice emerge from it

even though you are not there.

i am reminded of you at moments least expected
and it is as if my heart stops and beats faster all at once.

and just like that, it will disappear
like warm breath on a starlit winter night.

everything
i am is
nothing
without you.

i am a
shadow
without
a body.

i am a
silhouette
without
a frame of skin.

i am a
gust of wind
without the air
to carry me.

i am a
sunset without
even a single moment
to follow.

there was something about the way your face would light up when you had a story you wanted to tell me. a certain kind of radiance that i had never quite seen before. it was as if you were excited to hear yourself form the words, and for me to hear them for the very first time. your voice rang at a higher octave and with an exuberance in your cadence. with narratives, both big and small, it was like i was being taken on a tour of the cathedral built within you. a celestial dome sheathed in renaissance paintings and stained glass windows and the aroma of burning incense. on one such visit, the grandeur of your mind was only further magnified when i came upon a little girl playing right there in the center of it all. i introduced myself and shook her hand. she asked if i would stay awhile and so i did. as i sat down beside her, she showed me her doll and told me about all the journeys they had been on together. she brushed its hair so meticulously as if to make the words you spoke to me all the more clear. and it did. i understood it all then and i was spellbound. so i sat there for a little while longer before she took off for her next adventure.

your body
stood glorious in its grace.

your eyes
saw through all my stumbling follies.

your smile
enraptured me beyond my will.

your mind
mesmerized my every musing.

your soul
healed me into a euphoric daze.

your song
softly strumming along the heartstrings

in all that i am.

you carried summer on your skin
but winter in your heart.
oh, how i did fall for you anyway
as you brought the spring to my soul
for however brief it was before
our seasons changed.

on the evening of her leaving, i unveiled myself before the dark autumn night and breathed in the cold air long enough to extinguish the fire in my lungs so that i could bellow out to the sky, "but i gave her everything i had to give!"

the wind was coy for a moment, but it had heard my calling. as it stirred itself into a whisper, it brushed against my ear, "but what you had was not enough."

just then, lightning cracked its whip through the faint of clouds and a flood of rain came pouring down. it bled and blended itself with the tears streaming down my cheeks, together stirring into an ocean of despair filling around my feet. i dropped to my knees and they clashed against the sinking earth.

with my head in my hands, i sobbed with the world's most tragic display of frailty. for deep down inside, i knew that on the other end of the axis there was a sun demanding that i stand back up, and that what i really needed to do was to start standing taller. the voice inside reminded, "never let her see you like this, because she will forget why she ever fell in love with you at all."

the well from which i drink
now only stews with fire.
where am i to quench my thirst
for a taste of you?
how will i quell this writhing tongue
which only ever wished to speak your name?

the demons within
could not stand a fighting chance
in the presence of your light.
your soul was like an inferno
by which they were burned and buried.
you were a quietus to their quarrels.
a ravaging to their reprisals.
but when i lost you,
they resurrected themselves
from the ashes of your ardor
and there was no shield nor armor,
no weapon i could wield
that would subdue the war they waged.
they knew i was vulnerable to their vengeance
for i was in love with another who no longer loved me.

there was a whole ocean of you
that lived inside my chest
but i had not the faintest notion
it stirred within me
until you were gone
and the wild tide
of its salted waters
crashed through the shore
of my crestfallen eyes.

"i think i just fell in love with the idea of you,"
she said.
there and then,
i could feel myself morph into
a phantasm of my former self.
the me i knew began to vanish.
anything i could have said then
would have been nothing more than an echo of itself.
so i dissolved into silence
and i have moved through this world like the mist ever since.
what else is a man to do
when the woman he loves tells him that
he is not enough?
i am not saying that it is right.
i am just saying that this is what happened.
and there is no moral to be found here.

inside of me
you tilled a garden but did not stay to tend to it.
look now at what i have become.
entangled and entwined
by all the ways i tried to reach for the sun.
dead roots flooded by unrelenting rains.
limp and overgrown from a failure to flourish.
jagged and jilted
from the friction of passing chances.
as we grew further apart,
i too grew of thorny weeds and bleeding fruits
and aging bark against the asphyxiating vines.
i am menacing and wild.
these leaves of your abandon come through now in my eyes
and through my fingertips and in the words i speak.
and all around, others are afraid.
they innately know it is better
to forgo the fire of the raging woods
for the gentle waves of the paved roads.

these static nights are
swooning with the song
of every word you spoke
and the sound of your seductive voice
spinning in endless circles.
slowly serenading the dark spaces
etched inside my mind
with a needle lightly against the crevices
that it had intended to find.

but the record keeps on skipping

but the record keeps on skipping

but the record keeps on skipping

...

i try to find you in shadows of wine
swirling at the bottom of a bottle
and in apparitions of smoke
escaping from my lungs.
breathless and intoxicated
on a hopeless journey to catch a glimpse of you
that would satiate my grieving soul.
and the ground will begin to spin
beneath my feet
and the ceiling will begin to shift
above my head
and my legs will forget how to stand
and i will fall down
into the blackness behind my eyes.
but it is okay
because i am just a moment away
where i will begin dreaming of you
even if i never remember when i awake.

you were a cause calling me to champion—
a fight worthy of my fist.
with an undying rise,
i would have shielded you
if for nothing but one last embrace.

but as i lay face down on this reddened field,
mouth silenced by the dirt it eats,
i must not betray my conscious
and confront a thought that still beats

in unison with my withering breath
(even though my heart might feel it untrue)
that it may have been better to have never loved at all
than for my spirit to die this death eternally loving you.

this is my only triumph: that i fought like a man with nothing more to lose. a magnificent spectacle of shortcomings, of clumsy sprinting toward a line that kept on retracting into the furthering distance – stoically sacrificing my own pride as i left only the shed skin of myself behind – trapped inside the very chest of treasure that i explored to find. now i look at my reflection in a shattered mirror and ask, "what have i become?"

it answers back: a bee stuck in its own honey. a vagabond caught in quicksand who sinks deeper the harder he tries to escape it. an insect swarming ecstatically toward a flood of light only for it to be the very thing that would burn him maimed. a bewildering death of who i was in pursuit of who i thought you wanted me to be.

this victory is mine alone to hold true: that i failed myself more than i ever failed you.

…and then i came to think that
perhaps we could be broken together,
and the pieces that fell away from me
would rise into the spaces of you…

oblivious to the obvious,
you could not see the man standing before you

whose only desire was to walk by your side
and only ever wanted to help you on your way.

how ironic it was you were always so cautious
not to get lost in my eyes
that you could not realize
the one you sought was the one you found.

i so deeply wish
you would have allowed me to love you
in the way that you longed to be loved.

as much as i am shattered by the breaking of us,
struggling to pick up the pieces of what fell (in love),
i feel even more sorrow for you.
for you gave back all the love i gave
because you believed you did not deserve it.

but now i want to break through
your façade of hostile disappointment,
and pierce through all those acerbic words
you spoke, which i will never resent you for,
so that i may tell you as lovingly as i always did…

                              you. deserve. it.

you deserve to have another forget himself
when he is in your presence,
to have his hand feel hollow
when not holding yours,
to have another who restlessly
travels through miles of sleep
so that he can awaken back to you.

                              you. deserve. it.

but, alas, never again from me.
so i will lament the loss of all you stole from yourself,
and reconcile the fact that those moments with you
that seemed to drift on forever passed by too fast,
and that you were the most enchanting being that
i have ever come to know, and will never know again.

and
to the one who should ever come to have any feeling
for this broken shell of a man who stands before her,
whose head is hung so low to the ground
that he cannot seem to look up long enough
to see another equally deserving of the same,
i apologize from the bottom of my broken heart…

                              none. deserve. this.

i met your every cloud
with the warmth of my sun
and every flood you raged
with the dam of my surrendering hands.
each clap of your thunder was always
silenced by the stillness of my somber skies.
but i could never really quell the nature
of the storm that lived within you—
the one that brought cold rain
to our every summer morning
and unforgiving scorched air
to the lungs of our fevered love.

no moon of mine could ever change this tide.

peculiar were the ways
how i found a reason
for the chaos.
in the aftermath of you,
i tried to calculate
all the ways you may have thought
i was not good enough

and then became it.

i hoped that at one point the tears i wept would have
revived the ethereal flower we once blossomed together.

in perpetual echoes, from the deepest skies, i am urged to ask:
how did i come to be capsized in such stagnant waters?

how could it be that the one who was closest to my heart
was always just beyond the furthest reaches of my arms?

i sharpen all these words of despair
                         with the edges of my own teeth
                                   only to swallow them.

like reaching for the stars
only to catch a handful of clouds,

i wanted to find the infinite with you,
yet all we found was the way we end.

but if i had read your eyes more closely,
i would have seen that the story they told of us

was always written in past tense.

on my tongue
still sits all the things
i never got a chance to say:
words which might
have made you stay.

and there is not a single sound
left in the echoes of my
barely beating chest
that does not drum the rhythm
of its own heartbreak,

hoping that you will hear them
and find your way back to
                              me.

alas, i knew only a sliver of you—
the silver contour to a crescent moon.
your eyes reflected the bluest skies—
but clouded from the fallen dreams
of those who came before.
...those whose sins i was destined to pay...
it was always your coldest words that burned me the most.
but you could have blinded me of my sight,
freed me from the cage of my ribs,
unsewn me from my sinews,
and even then i would have crawled through the dark
to find my way back to you
because, despite it all, you were
the only thing that ever made me feel so fiercely alive.
carved on my heart
is your image
with the most rusted blunt of blades.

when i close my eyes,
i see you everywhere
and i want to sleep there

forever.

but when i lay awake
and the constellations are in full bloom,
drawing out a map to a destiny
that never came to be,
i perseverate on the past—
the mornings of your head buried in my chest.
the mournings of my head buried in my hands.
i mutter to myself with a muddied whisper,

"i am still trying to forget you."

these lips which once found a home
with your midnight kisses
are now left orphaned
only with lonely questions of "why?"
from pillow thoughts and timid prayers
before a brooding sky
and the cold air they now breathe
only ever seems to answer with a sigh.

while the world went on
armored and afraid
with their fragile egos
in continuous jeopardy
of nothing and everything,
i dove heartfirst into the possibility of us.
gave all of myself to you completely
with not ever a question
if what we had was true.
i never wanted to come to learn of
the wisdom in their foolish ways
but i do.

naive it was for me to think
you would offer your hand
to pull me back to the air,
as i was engulfed lower
                        and
                                lower into the swallows,
when it was you for whom i was drowning to save.

there are flashes of lucidity
that appear unsuspectingly

when i realize i may be romanticizing the memory of you–
idealizing us into something greater than we were–

stitching all our moments of felicity
into a fold that blinds me from the reality.

but it does not mean that i miss you any less.
            no, i do not miss you any less.

each time the great swell compels me to cry,
the tears fall always from the weight of you.
no matter how distant the failure,
no matter how disconnected the fear,

it. is. always. you.

and again, here we are not. two strangers lost in paradise.
estranged but chained by the memories that remain.

when was it i was to forget you?
what was it i was holding on to?

you have long since released me from your grip,
                                   but still i am not free…

the most sacred verses
i have of you to speak
are not in words.
they are uttered
in shudders of breath
before i weep.
they are in a language
scribed by tired eyes.
inked on parchment
like dead tears on a pillow.

what good is it to have these two hands
if they are not here to catch you.
you are a creature of flight.
an angel with wings.
the sky loves you
too much to
allow you
to fall
but
i
keep
looking
up
to
find
you
anyway.

it could have been as simple as, "goodbye."
it could have been as easy as, "i am sorry."
it could have all been put back together with,
                                    "can we start again?"

i wish i would have found
more reasons to hold you closer
while i still had the chance.
a cobbled road to walk along.
a vast horizon to sit before.
a leap into a summer lake from a tall branch on a tree.
a dip into an autumn sea before a warming sunrise.
of all the things,
this is my greatest regret.

countless
encounters
to
arrive
at
you
and
it
is
only
you
who
still
remains.

this road
back to myself
is too long,
too quiet,
and too dark.

how was it
that i drifted
so far
just to stand
next to you?

why is that
every step
i take
feels further away
from the truth?

this road
apart from you
is too long,
too quiet,
and too dark.

i have grown numb
looking for you in places
where i will never find you.
i am defeated into surrender,
drunk with unrequited love,
tucked in for a listless slumber.
with my head against the dust,
i look up to the open sky–
the only thread that is left
stitched between you and me–
and blow it a kiss goodnight.

it is not that i will never know
joy
or
love
or
bliss
or
contentment,

it is that i will never know
the
sound
of
your
laughter
again
and that to me was everything.

on rainy sunday afternoons,
i peer outside against the windowsill
of what was once the steamy pane that
shielded our wildness from the wilderness
and watch as every missed moment
accrues into drip drops on the glass
trickling down into the trail of another.

i envy the waters for their daring of flow
and the simple ease by which they let each other go.

there is so much extraordinary suffering
in the dark spaces of this sullied world.

who am i to know such joy?
why should i ask for more?

a true man does not demand
more than what he deserves.

it is only fair then that i should lose her.
reasonable to expect our sun would set.

that a night should come where
my lips would never meet hers again.

i stumble over shards of you
everywhere i go.
each one biting at my feet,
tripping my step,
leaving a crimson trail of me behind.

i try to break past the promise of our future
as i bleed myself alive.

but there are times,
after a long storm of tears,
when i am able to stop the whirling winds
of my own melancholy
by drawing it all into my breath.

in an instant,
i am calmed and quieted.

my heart slows to a restful rhythm
because i come to ponder
that perhaps
i have taken in a part of the air
that you out there
may have touched.

i suppose what i needed most

was for her to love herself more
so that she could love me.

it was the unlocking of her cage
that would have set us free.

i only wish i could have conjured
the words, the wisdom, or a world

that might have given her the key.

i have not come looking for you
not because i do not care

but because i have come to learn
in ever so tragic ways

that those who have wings
do not belong to me

but were made to fly
and meant for the air.

so i will remember us
for the both of us.

such a spectacular light show
as i recall it to be

deserves to live on among the stars.

perhaps it was as inevitable
as the infinite shadow play
of the sun and the moon,
perpetually polarized
in an eclipse of each other's light,
that our flames shall never merge
to burn brighter together
because i am simply
not the man i need to be
to have the woman i want to hold.

my love, my sweet, my true...

you were not just a star in the sky.
you were the whole wide sky entirely.
the vast expanse of my gaze
swirling in shapes, colors, and sounds.

and i tried so desperately to transcend mere words
so that i could express what it really was in my heart to say:
something a thousand times the power of "i love you."

but i failed to do so every time.
i fail to do so every time.

we scoff at the idea of ghosts—
too childish for the grown to affirm.
but i can tell you that they are real.

i am haunted always by the memories
of the woman i loved,
the moments we shared,
and the mistakes we made
to lose each other.

and she is as real to me now
as when she was in my arms.

it would be so much easier
if i could just blame you for it all.
catalog each vitriolic syllable that escaped your lips.
alphabetize every mistake you made.
map out every wrong turn you took.
cast you as a villain and myself your victim.
but none of this would be true
because i did so truly love you.
and as i lay rest to the remains,
i know that you did too.

it was a long and defiant rain,
but today i woke up to the rising sun
and felt the same pulse in my veins
as when i would wake up next to you.
i stepped out onto the grass—
soles slick against the morning dew—

soil emergent with the air of petrichor.
two squirrels playing a game that
only lovers would ever understand.

for a moment this morning, i did not mourn.
i celebrated you in all that surrounds.

when all was said
and all was done,
i was just a boy
on a swing
who wanted
to hold hands
with the girl
next to him,
thinking we
would reach higher
if we could ride the sky together.

i know in my heart
that the ways of this world
are governed by the laws of karma.
and so when i weep,
i may wilt the future that lays before you.

for what goes around comes around
and the pain we cause in others
will one day become
the weight we too shall bear.

for this reason alone,
i will let it all go,
find a way to move on,
and summon the strength
to stand back up.

wherever you are,
i hope you are not like me.
i hope you do not remember us.
i want you to go on breathing—
living a new life happily.

this loneliness—
i know i can conquer
        (not with you here)
with my one hand
clasping the other.

on this mortal level
of lower frequencies,
insecurities hem webs
too hermetic to unravel.

so i will lay down
and look up
and call upon the divine
with a humble tongue.

solemn and silent—
before the great unknown,
        (communing with you there)
i will transcend the air to where
all souls are sewn together as one.

every language in the world has a word for love—
                drifting across seas and skies—
                even more than i know to name.

but there is only one love for which i was ever fluent,
                and it was
                you.

and to describe that which i felt,
                well my dear,
                for that there are no words.

but i will keep writing to find them anyway—
                these words, words, words,
                words...

praying they will pave a path for my heart
                to one day finally find
                its way back home.

the earth was never as soft
as it was when i
laid against it with you

to imbibe the oceans of sky,
which imbued us renewed
with a love we knew was true.

enamored by the midnight's hue,
our fingers traced
an astral path to a time

where our vision for
each other could blur askew
into one harmonious line.

and the air was never as sweet
as the swallow i drew
from the kiss of your lips.

and the moon never
illumined as brightly
as when reflected from our eyes.

and never will there be a moment
that i will cherish more
than that singular expanse of infinity.

you. me. we. us.

how are you supposed to love a butterfly?

you hold your arms open like a panoply of wind
awaiting them beyond the chrysalis.
and when they emerge,
present your chest as a field of milkweed.
hold yourself firm as they eat with their feet.
never fault them for the treads they leave upon you.
give them your heart
with one part nectar and one part water.

and then you wait.
and then you pray.
you wait to see if she will fly away.
you pray that she will stay.
and no matter what she decides,
never let your love run astray.
for she is a creature of wings,
and she may come back one day.

each page is a fallen petal
that i lay down at the feet of your fading memory
and as it grows more difficult to remember
the story we shared,
i find solace in the hope
that perhaps in another life
we shall meet again
to write another one
with a different ending.

NEALSEHGAL.COM

E
L
E
G
Y

F
O
R

A

B
U
T
T
E
R
F
L
Y

Made in the USA
Middletown, DE
18 February 2019